Cookbook

Favorite family recipes from
Out Here readers across America

Designed by Amy Ware, Locomotion Creative
Edited by Carol Davis, *Out Here* magazine
Food photography by Mark Mosrie and John Walker
Lifestyle photography by Greg Latza
Food styling by Whitney Kemp

TractorSupply.com

The Out Here Cookbook

Favorite family recipes from *Out Here* readers across America

Tradition has always been an important part of Tractor Supply Co.'s *Out Here* magazine since it debuted in 2003. We've featured soapmakers, farms that have remained in the same family for multiple generations, and old-time music makers.

Some of the deepest traditions, however, can be found in the kitchen, where families continue to share some of the same dishes that their grandparents and great-grandparents enjoyed decades before. There's something comfortable and familiar in recipes that have been handed down time and time again.

So we knew that "Favorite Family Recipes" — *your* favorite family recipes — would always be a part of *Out Here* magazine. Each issue contains five recipes from among the hundreds submitted by our readers, including flavorful main dishes, comforting casseroles, desserts that will delight you, and much, much more.

Now, you can have many of these family favorites with the latest volume in the *Out Here Cookbook* series.

When you share them with your family, you'll see why they've stood the test of time.

Baked Oatmeal

Those who normally don't care for oatmeal will love this "hearty country breakfast cake," writes Rhoda B., of Goshen, Ind. Make it even more convenient by mixing it the evening before and refrigerating until morning, she suggests.

½ cup butter, melted
1 cup brown sugar
2 eggs
3 cups quick oats
2 tsp. baking powder
1 tsp. salt
1 cup milk
1 apple, chopped
¼ cup raisins
Cinnamon to taste

① Mix the first seven ingredients together well.
② Add chopped apple and raisins.
③ Spread in greased 9x13 pan or individual-sized baking dishes and sprinkle cinnamon over top.
④ Bake at 350 degrees for 20-30 minutes.
⑤ Serve warm.

Serves 10-12.

Grammy's Waffles

The cornmeal in her grandmother's waffle recipe seems to be the ingredient that makes them so good, writes Gigi G., of Catlett, Va.

"Best we can tell, the recipe is over 102 years old and it is the best!" she writes.

2 cups flour
¼ cup yellow cornmeal
½ tsp. salt
3 tsp. baking powder
1 tsp. baking soda
2 eggs, separated
2 cups buttermilk or sour milk
6 Tbsp. vegetable oil

① Sift together dry ingredients. Set aside.
② Add egg yolks to buttermilk and oil. Beat slightly.
③ Add dry ingredients to liquid all at once and beat with rotary mixer until batter is smooth.
④ Beat egg whites until stiff peaks form. Fold egg whites into batter very gently.
⑤ Pour batter into a pitcher and do not stir afterward.
⑥ Pour onto heated waffle iron and cook as directed.

Serves 4.

Blueberry French Toast

Jane V., of Orrtanna, Pa., offers French toast with a twist.
"It's a hearty breakfast casserole and very delicious," she writes.

12 slices day-old white bread,
   crusts removed
2 8-oz. packages cream cheese
1 cup blueberries, fresh or frozen
12 eggs
2 cups milk
⅓ cup maple syrup or honey

Sauce:
1 cup sugar
2 Tbsp. cornstarch
1 cup water
1 cup blueberries, fresh or frozen
1 Tbsp. butter or margarine

① Tear or cut bread into 1-inch cubes and place half in a greased baking dish.
② Cut cream cheese into 1-inch cubes and place over bread.
③ Top with blueberries and remaining bread.
④ In large bowl, beat eggs.
⑤ Add milk and syrup (or honey); mix well and pour over bread mixture. Cover and chill overnight.
⑥ Remove from refrigerator 30 minutes before baking, then cover and bake for 30 minutes at 350 degrees.
⑦ Uncover and bake 25-30 minutes more or until golden brown.

Sauce:
① In a saucepan, combine sugar and cornstarch.
② Add water and bring to a boil over medium heat; boil for 3 minutes, stirring constantly.
③ Stir in blueberries, reduce heat, and simmer for 8-10 minutes or until blueberries have burst.
④ Stir in butter until melted.
⑤ Serve over French toast.

Serves 6-8.

Cottage Cheese Pancakes

"This is a great way for kids to have plenty of protein for breakfast as you are getting them off to school," writes Lonna F., of Brooksville, Fla. *"It is also a terrific way to use up old cottage cheese."*

She also suggests doubling the recipe to keep the extra pancakes in the refrigerator for quick snacks.

4 eggs
¼ tsp. salt
1 cup cottage cheese
2 Tbsp. oil
1 cup flour, sifted

① Mix all ingredients in a blender and blend on low speed until cheese curds disappear.
② Pour enough batter onto medium-heated griddle to make 4-inch pancakes.
③ Cook a minute or two and turn when nicely browned. Cook until both sides are nicely browned and the pancake is cooked through.
④ Serve immediately with butter and syrup or your favorite pancake topping.

Yields 8-10 pancakes.

Three-Minute Fruit Dish

Children love this breakfast because they get to add a carbonated soft drink, says Sharon C., of Grand Junction, Mich.

2 cups banana, sliced in rounds
2 cups apple, sliced in thin wedges
2 cups fresh blueberries
2 cups orange juice
7-Up soft drink
Pecans, chopped

① Combine the first four ingredients; set aside.
② When ready to serve, have each person add 7-Up and chopped pecans to taste to their own serving.

Serves 6.

Ham 'n Eggs Brunch Braid

Karen W., of Elk River, Minn., who got this recipe from her daughter, loves it because it is so versatile. If her guest doesn't like ham, she'll substitute with sausage or bacon.

"You can pretty much throw anything in," she says. "It depends on who's eating."

4 oz. cream cheese	2 Tbsp. onions, sliced
½ cup milk	1 tsp. butter
8 eggs, 1 separated	2 8-oz. packages refrigerated
¼ tsp. salt	crescent rolls
Dash pepper	¼ lb. chopped ham
¼ cup red bell pepper, chopped	2 oz. cheddar cheese, shredded

① Preheat oven to 375 degrees.

② Place cream cheese and milk in bowl, microwave on high 1 minute, then whisk until smooth.

③ Separate 1 egg, reserve the egg white. Add the yolk and the remaining 7 eggs, salt, and pepper and whisk.

④ Add bell pepper and onions to the egg mixture.

⑤ Melt butter in pan, then add the egg mixture. Cook over low heat, until the eggs are set but still moist.

⑥ Open and unroll crescent dough, but do not pull apart perforations. On a baking pan, place the dough side by side and pinch together at edge to create a single 12x15 sheet of dough. Tuck underneath.

⑦ Along the longest edges of dough, cut strips 1½ inches wide and 3 inches long.

⑧ Arrange ham evenly over middle of dough. Spoon eggs over the ham, then sprinkle cheddar cheese over the eggs.

⑨ Braid by lifting strips of dough across the filling to meet at the center, twisting each strip one turn. Brush dough lightly with beaten egg white using a pastry brush.

⑩ Bake 25-28 min. or until deep golden brown. Cut into slices and serve. Yields 10 servings.

Baked Eggs in Maple Toast Cups

Trase P., of Fenton, Mich., found this recipe in one of the hundreds of vintage cookbooks that she's collected.

"It's a good one for when you have an influx of eggs in the spring," she says, noting that they have about 70 chickens and ducks.

She, in fact, prefers duck eggs in this recipe — "They have more of a buttery, rich taste" — but her husband prefers chicken eggs.

2 Tbsp. maple syrup or maple-flavored syrup
2 Tbsp. butter
6 slices dense, soft white bread
6 eggs

① Preheat oven to 400 degrees.

② Spray muffin pan with non-stick spray.

③ Melt butter and syrup together in microwave-proof dish for about 30 seconds. Stir the butter into the syrup so it melts completely.

④ Cut crusts off of bread and roll them flat with a rolling pin.

⑤ Brush each slice on one side with syrup mixture and press into a cup of the muffin pan, with dry side down, syrup side up.

⑥ Break one egg into each cup. Season with salt and pepper.

⑦ Bake for 15 minutes for soft-boiled texture, or 20 minutes to set the eggs firmer.

⑧ After removing from the oven, run a butter knife around the perimeter of each cup and then use two forks to pull each cup out.

⑨ Serve with additional syrup-butter mixture if desired.

Serves 6.

Option: "You can also sprinkle crumbled cooked bacon in the bottom of each of the bread cups before adding the egg, if it suits your taste," Trace says.

Summer Salsa

Dawn M. of Glasgow, Ky., made this fresh summer salsa especially for her husband, because it was one of his favorites, she says.

1 clove garlic
2 tsp. kosher salt, divided
4 medium ripe tomatoes, cored and diced
¼ medium red onion, finely diced
1 jalapeño pepper, stemmed and minced (with seeds for more heat)
¼ cup fresh cilantro, chopped
White corn tortilla chips, for dipping

① Smash the garlic clove, sprinkle with 1 tsp. salt, and, with the flat side of a large knife, mash and smear the mixture to a coarse paste.

② Combine the garlic mixture, tomatoes, onion, jalapeño, and cilantro in a serving bowl.

③ Season with the remaining 1 tsp. salt, adding more to taste, if necessary.

④ Serve immediately with tortilla chips (or use as a burger topping), or to allow the flavors to blend, cover and set aside for one hour at room temperature.

Serves 4-6.

Cheese Ball

Mildred G.'s mother-in-law at the time gave this cheeseball recipe to her about 40 years ago. "It is quite a hit at parties and get-togethers," writes Mildred, of Kingsbury, Texas. "You can't stop eating it!"

She notes that you can substitute the honey ham ingredient for chicken, turkey, beef, or plain ham.

2 8-oz. packages cream cheese, slightly softened
5-6 green onions (including tops), sliced
2 2-oz. packages honey ham, finally chopped
3 tsp. Accent all-natural flavor enhancer
3 tsp. Worcestershire sauce
Crackers

① Mix all ingredients thoroughly.
② Mold into a ball and serve with crackers.

Barbecued Meatballs

The key to this tasty recipe is the homemade barbecue sauce, writes Chris M., of Union City, Tenn. "The secret is in the sauce; don't cut corners by using bottled barbecue sauce," she writes.

Meatballs:
3 lbs. ground beef
1 12-oz. can evaporated milk
1 cup oats
1 cup cracker crumbs
2 eggs
½ cup onion, finely chopped
½ tsp. garlic powder
2 tsp. salt
½ tsp. pepper
2 tsp. chili powder

Sauce:
4 cups ketchup
2 cups brown sugar
1 tsp. liquid smoke, or to taste
1 tsp. garlic powder
½ cup onion, chopped

① To make meatballs, combine all ingredients (mixture will be soft) and shape into walnut-size balls. Place meatballs in a single layer on wax paper-lined cookie sheets; freeze until solid. Store frozen meatballs in freezer bags until ready to cook.

② To make sauce, combine all ingredients and stir until sugar is dissolved. Place frozen meatballs in 13x9-inch baking pans, and pour on the sauce. Bake at 350 degrees for 1 hour.

Yields 80 meatballs.

Cook's notes: This recipe can easily be halved to make just 40 meatballs and half the sauce.

Creamy Broccoli Soup

"This soup, made with Minute Rice and fresh broccoli is wholesome, flavorful, and easy," writes Denise P., of Bainbridge, Ohio. *"Serve with breadsticks and a side salad, and you have a complete meal."*

2 medium carrots, chopped
1 medium onion, chopped
2 celery stalks, chopped
3 Tbsp. oil
3 cups chicken broth
2 cups water
2 small bunches fresh broccoli, trimmed, cut into 3-inch lengths (about 4½ cups)
½ cup Minute Rice, uncooked
2 cups milk
¼ cup grated Parmesan cheese
Salt and pepper to taste

① Stir carrots, onion, and celery in hot oil in large saucepan on medium-high heat for 3 minutes.
② Add chicken broth and water; stir. Bring to boil.
③ Stir in broccoli and rice and reduce heat to medium-low; simmer 10-15 minutes or until vegetables are tender, stirring frequently.
④ Add mixture in batches, to blender or food processor; cover. Blend until slightly pureed.
⑤ Return soup to pot. Add milk and cheese; continue to cook until heated through, stirring occasionally.

Serves 6-8.

Cook's notes: Add 4½ cups frozen peas for additional color.

Autumn Chowder

Carla S., of Aberdeen, S.D., and her family love this tasty chowder at holidays and get-togethers. "Hopefully you and your readers will enjoy them also. Enjoy!" she writes.

2 bacon strips, diced
¼ cup onion, chopped
1 medium red potato, diced
1 small carrot, halved lengthwise and thinly sliced
½ cup water
¾ tsp. chicken bouillon granules
1 cup milk
⅔ cup frozen corn
⅛ tsp. pepper
2½ tsp. all-purpose flour
2 Tbsp. cold water
¾ cup shredded cheddar cheese

① In a saucepan, cook bacon over medium heat until crisp; remove to paper towels. Drain, reserving 1 tsp. drippings.

② In the drippings, sauté onion until tender. Add the potato, carrot, water, and bouillon. Bring to a boil. Reduce heat; cover and simmer for 15-20 minutes or until the vegetables are almost tender.

③ Stir in milk, corn, and pepper. Cook 5 minutes longer.

④ Combine flour and cold water until smooth; gradually whisk into soup. Bring to a boil; cook and stir for 1-2 minutes or until thickened.

⑤ Remove from the heat; stir in cheese until melted. Sprinkle with bacon.

Serves 2-3.

Spicy Chicken Tortilla Soup

This spicy soup is an original by Tom and Pat T. of Manton, Mich. "We developed this recipe through trial and error," they write. "It is a favorite with our family and friends."

1 medium onion
1 clove garlic
2 Tbs. vegetable oil
3 cans chicken broth
1 tsp. cayenne pepper
¾ tsp. basil
1 tsp. cilantro
½ tsp. salt
¼ tsp. pepper
1 15-oz. can tomato sauce
2 cups cooked chicken, chopped

Topping:
Tortilla chips
Monterey Jack shredded cheese
Sour cream
Avocados

① Sauté onion and garlic.
② Add the remainder of the ingredients.
③ Bring to a boil then reduce heat to a simmer (Can be served immediately).
④ In each serving bowl, crumble up ¼ cup of tortilla chips and top with shredded cheese.
⑤ Pour soup into bowl.
⑥ Top soup with one large chip, a dab of sour cream, and slice of avocado.

Yields four 1½-cup servings.

Cook's notes: We recommend doubling this recipe.

Cowboy Steak & Veggie Soup

Robyn C., of Wilmington, Ohio, found this recipe in a newspaper more than 20 years ago, but quickly made it her own by changing up the ingredients to better suit her family's tastes. "We know what we like," she says.

You can do the same, she says, by adding ingredients that your family likes.

1 lb. boneless beef sirloin steak about 1 inch thick
1 tsp. dried basil leaves
½ tsp. salt
¼ tsp. pepper
2 cloves garlic, crushed
1 Tbsp. oil
2 14.5-oz. cans beef broth
1 16-oz. jar chunky salsa
1 lb. package frozen soup mix vegetables of your choice
1 15.5-oz. can Great Northern beans
Fresh basil and parsley to taste

① Cut beef into ¼ inch strips, or into your preferred size. In medium bowl, combine beef, basil, salt, pepper, garlic, and oil. Toss to coat.
② Heat Dutch oven over medium high heat until hot. Add beef mixture. Cook and stir until browned.
③ Stir in broth, salsa, vegetables, beans, basil, and parsley. Bring to boil.
④ Reduce heat to low. Simmer 10 minutes.

Serves 6-8.

Spinach Salad

Judi D., of Russellville, Tenn., first tried this recipe more than 25 years ago when her next-door neighbor in Pennsylvania served it, and she's stuck to the original ingredients. "I kind of like things simple and basic," she says. "Sometimes if you add too much stuff to recipes, you don't get the flavor of everything."

1 lb. washed fresh spinach
Fresh mushrooms to taste, chopped
6 large green onions, chopped
1 clove garlic, chopped
4 hard-boiled eggs, chopped
8 slices fried bacon, crumbled

Dressing:
½ tsp. salt
½ cup oil
¼ cup vinegar
3 tsp. lemon juice

① Mix dressing ingredients; set aside.
② Toss first four ingredients together. Add dressing ingredients to salad and toss.
③ Let sit ½ hour before serving.
④ Add eggs and bacon just before serving.

Serves 6-8.

Carrot Salad

Sharon M. received her carrot salad recipe from her mother-in-law many years ago.

"She was a good cook," writes Sharon, of Richlandtown, Pa. "This was one of my favorites, and my family loves it, too. It goes well with picnic food or any food.

1 lb. carrots, sliced ¼ inch and cooked
½ green pepper, chopped
¼-½ medium red onion, chopped

Dressing:
⅓ cup extra virgin olive oil
¼ cup vinegar
2 Tbsp. honey (or sugar)
1½ tsp. salt

① Mix cooked carrots, green pepper and red onion together.
② Whisk together all dressing ingredients.
③ Add dressing to vegetables.
④ Refrigerate. This keeps well in the refrigerator.

Serves 4-6.

Crunchy Wild Rice Salad

"My family enjoys this as a different and refreshing salad," writes Deanna J., of Mound Valley, Kan. *"When I take it to dinners, someone always asks for the recipe. I hope your readers enjoy it."*

1 6-oz. package long-grain and wild rice mix
1 10-oz. package frozen peas, thawed or fresh
1 cup celery, fresh or frozen, chopped
⅓ cup green bell peppers, fresh or frozen, chopped
5 green green onions, fresh or frozen, chopped
½ cup Ranch dressing
1 cup (4 oz.) cheddar cheese, shredded

① Cook rice according to package directions.
② Stir in peas. Cool.
③ Combine celery and next three ingredients.
④ Pour over rice mixture and gently stir.
⑤ Cover and chill for at least 4 hours.
⑥ Stir in cheese just before serving.

Makes about 7 cups.

Baked Salmon and Asparagus

Erica E., of Cross Plains, Ind., makes this dish for her family at least once a week. "Even our kids love it and ask for seconds! It's delicious, simple, and healthy, too," she writes.

2 unbreaded salmon fillets
Asparagus stalks
1 stick butter or margarine, melted
1 tsp. black pepper
1 tsp. garlic salt
1 Tbsp. garlic flakes
1 lemon
1 Tbsp. parsley flakes

① Preheat oven to 375 degrees.

② Place salmon fillets in a 9x13-inch no-stick sprayed pan. Lay asparagus stalks in pan around fillets.

③ Brush melted butter or margarine generously over entire dish. Sprinkle on black pepper, garlic salt, and garlic flakes. Squeeze entire lemon over salmon and top it all off with parsley flakes.

④ Place in the oven and check every 5 minutes for 12-15 minutes until salmon is dark pink to slightly golden on the outside, opaque inside, and asparagus is tender.

⑤ Remove when cooked and serve immediately over your favorite rice and with some fresh sliced tomatoes on the side.

Serves 2.

Grandma's Red Beans and Rice

Jimmy S. of Rosharon, Texas, loves this dish from his grandmother. "My grandmother was born and raised in Louisiana and she passed her cooking on to my mom and aunts," he says. "They are all great cooks."

1 yellow onion, diced
Black pepper to taste
Creole seasoning
1 large bag red kidney or pinto beans
Seasoning salt
Red pepper flakes
1 four-pack smoked ham hocks
Rice

① Fill a medium-sized pot with water just over halfway.
② Bring to a boil, add onion, black pepper, and 5 or 6 shakes Creole seasoning.
③ Add beans and 2 shakes of both seasoning salt and red pepper flakes.
④ Cover and cook for two hours. Beans will cook down two or three times, so watch and make sure you add enough water to keep beans covered.
⑤ The last time you add water, add smoked ham hocks and 2 or 3 shakes of Creole seasoning.
⑥ Cook for 30 more minutes.
⑦ Prepare rice according to the package.
⑧ Serve red beans and ham hock bits over rice.

Serves 10.

Louisiana-style Smothered Okra & Chicken

Jimmy S., of Rosharon, Texas, carries on a tasty, spicy family tradition with this Deep South dish.

1 chicken
Seasoning salt (He recommends Accent)
Salt and pepper to taste
1 yellow onion, diced
1 bell pepper, diced
1 clove garlic, chopped
2 links garlic sausage, cubed
1 48-oz. and 1 16-oz. bag of okra
1 16-oz. can tomato sauce
2 16-oz. cans hot Rotel tomatoes
1 bag of large shrimp
Rice

① Season chicken to taste with seasoning salt, salt, and pepper. Cook and dice.

② Coat large pot with vegetable oil and heat.

③ Add onion, bell pepper, and garlic. Cook for 5 minutes, add chicken. Stir until browned.

④ Add sausage and more vegetable oil, if needed. Cook for 15 minutes.

⑤ Add okra, salt, and pepper.

⑥ Add tomato sauce and ½ cup water. Cook for 15 minutes.

⑦ Add hot Rotel tomatoes and shrimp.

⑧ Add another ½ cup of water and 15 shakes of seasoning salt, and stir.

⑨ Slow cook for another 35 minutes.

⑩ Prepare rice according to package. Serve hot over rice.

Serves 10-12.

'Froggy Burger'

Adam P., of Jackson, Tenn., known as "Froggy" to his friends, has created a hamburger that's so popular among his friends that they've given it a name: The Froggy Burger.

"It's one that everybody comes back to. It's a hot burger and really spicy," he says. "Everybody loves it."

2 lbs. hamburger
2 eggs
1 bag of thick potato chips (he prefers Wavy Lay's)
1 Tbsp. garlic, minced
1 Tbsp. black pepper
1 Tbsp. red pepper, crushed
¼ cup red onion, minced
⅛ cup Italian seasoning
2 Tbsp. Worcestershire sauce
⅓ cup jalapeños, chopped

① Place hamburger in large bowl.

② Beat eggs and pour over hamburger.

③ Place a large handful or two of potato chips into a plastic sandwich bag and crush until you have about 1 cup of crushed chips. Use thick chips; thin ones don't add enough texture. Tortilla chips (such as Doritos) work well, too.

④ Add remaining ingredients and mix well.

⑤ Patty out four burgers and grill to taste.

Makes 4 burgers.

Tomato Pie

"A friend we met at the farmers' market shared this recipe with my family," writes Kacie V., of Mesick, Mich. *"It makes a delicious supper and it is so easy and simple."*

3 good-sized tomatoes
Sea salt
Freshly ground pepper
Pillsbury piecrust
1 cup basil, thinly chopped
2 cups mozzarella cheese, shredded
¼ cup extra light olive oil

① Thinly slice your tomatoes in rounds and others in halfrounds and lay them out on a few layers of paper towel to dry. Season them with sea salt and freshly ground pepper and let them sit for 20-30 minutes.

② Spread the piecrust in a shallow pan of any shape and bake the crust for 10-15 minutes at 300-325 degrees so the bottom gets a little brown. Let cool.

③ Place a thin layer of chopped basil to the baked crust.

④ Add shredded mozzarella cheese.

⑤ Arrange the tomatoes to fill the pan and drizzle ¼ cup or less of extra-light olive oil on top.

⑥ Bake at 325 degrees for 20-30 minutes. The cheese should be bubbling up through the tomatoes.

⑦ Let it sit for 30 minutes before you serve. Slice, then pop it back in the oven for a few minutes to serve it slightly warm.

Serves 4-6.

Spaghetti Sauce in Bulk

Annette W., of Mifflintown, Pa., remembers the days when members of her extended family gathered to make and preserve some 300 quarts — yes, you read that correctly — of spaghetti sauce each year.

"It's been a family recipe that we've used forever," she says. "Every year when my grandmother was still living, we would do it together because she had a humongous kitchen."

Everything was stored at Grandma's spacious home, as well, she says. "When you needed spaghetti sauce, you just went to Grandma's and got it."

½ bushel tomatoes
2 heads of garlic, chopped
1 hot pepper, chopped
3 green peppers, chopped
3 lbs. onions, chopped
1 pint oil
1½ cups sugar
½ cup salt
1 Tbsp. sweet basil
1 Tbsp. oregano
8 small cans tomato paste

① Thoroughly cook tomatoes and garlic together.
② Put mixture through a food mill (which mashes and sieves soft foods).
③ Cook peppers and onions in 1 pint of oil for 30 minutes. Drain.
④ Add everything to tomato mixture, including remaining ingredients.
⑤ Cook and stir to desired thickness.
⑥ Serve or preserve by either canning or freezing.

Makes about 7 quarts.

Terry's Salsa Meatloaf

Terry O., of Nashville, Tenn., puts an extra "zing" in her meatloaf by adding salsa.

1¾ - 2 lbs. hamburger meat
1 egg
1 16-oz. jar of your favorite chunky salsa
Garlic powder to taste (about 1 tsp.)
½ cup of quick oats
¾ cup wheat germ

① Combine all ingredients in a large bowl and mix thoroughly, preferably by hand.
② Place in loaf pan. If your loaf pans are smaller, divide and place in two loaf pans.
③ Bake at 375 degrees for 1 hour and 15 minutes.

Recipe options: Substitute ground turkey for beef; use more or less salsa in meat; and pour warmed salsa over a slice or two of meat when served.

Serves 6-8.

Rosemary Pork Loin with Cherry Sauce

Add something extra to your pork dishes with this simple, yet tasty, recipe from Tonya S., of Bradley, S.C. "It tastes great over cooked pork tenderloin," she writes.

Here's our recipe for pork tenderloin enhanced with Tonya's cherry sauce:

Rosemary Pork Loin:
1-1½ lb. pork tenderloin
1 clove garlic, minced
1 Tbsp. olive oil
1 Tbsp. balsamic vinegar
1 Tbsp. fresh rosemary, minced
1 tsp. salt
1 tsp. pepper

① Mix ingredients together and coat pork tenderloin; marinate at least two hours.

② When you're ready to cook, preheat oven to 350 degrees.

③ Cover tenderloin and bake for 50-55 minutes or until meat thermometer reaches 155 degrees.

④ After removing from oven, let tenderloin rest for 15 minutes before slicing and serving.

Serves 5-6.

Cherry Sauce:
2 cans drained pitted dark sweet red cherries, reserve liquid
Water
1 cup sugar
2 Tbsp. cornstarch
¼ tsp. salt
½ cup butter
2 cinnamon sticks
12 whole cloves
2 Tbsp. lemon juice

① In a 2-cup measuring cup, add water to reserved cherry juice liquid until equal to 1½ cups.

② In a 2-quart saucepan, combine sugar, cornstarch, and salt and add cherry liquid mixture.

③ Cook over medium heat, stirring occasionally until sugar is dissolved (1-2 minutes).

④ Stir in butter, cinnamon sticks, cloves, and lemon juice.

⑤ Continue cooking while stirring constantly until mixture thickens and comes to a full boil (4-6 minutes). Boil 1 minute.

⑥ Remove cinnamon sticks and cloves. Stir in cherries.

⑦ Pour over tenderloin.

Honey-Glazed Chicken

Fannie May M., of Holton, Mich., likes the mix of flavors in her honey-glazed chicken.

"We like the flavor with the honey and lemon juice; the sweet with the sour," she says. "It makes the chicken tangy."

½ cup flour
1 tsp. salt
½ tsp. red pepper
1 broiler frying chicken, cut up
½ cup butter, melted and divided
¼ cup brown sugar
¼ cup honey
¼ cup lemon juice
1 Tbsp. soy sauce (optional)
1½ tsp. curry powder

① Preheat oven to 350 degrees.
② In a bowl or bag, combine flour, salt, and pepper. Add chicken and dredge or shake to coat.
③ Pour 4 Tbsp. butter in a 9x13x2 pan. Place chicken in pan, turning pieces to coat.
④ Bake uncovered for 30 minutes.
⑤ Combine brown sugar, honey, lemon juice, soy sauce, curry powder, and remaining butter. Pour over chicken.
⑥ Bake 45 minutes more or until chicken is tender, basting several times with pan drippings.

Serves 4-6.

Granny's Crustless Turkey Pie

"After holidays at our house, the demand for next-day leftovers is almost equal to the holiday meal itself," writes Rita T., of Pottsville, Pa. "In this recipe, quite a few calories are saved by baking this mixture of old-fashioned flavors in a pie plate without a crust."

1 cup sweet onion, chopped
1 cup organic celery, finely diced
2 medium Granny Smith (or cooking) apples peeled, cored, and diced
24 oz. leftover turkey (or cooked chicken) cut in nugget-like pieces
2 cups cooked rice
½ tsp. curry powder
¼ tsp. ground black pepper
1 10¾-oz. can low-fat cream of celery soup, undiluted
1 10¾-oz. can low-sodium chicken broth
¼ cup part-skim cheese, shredded or grated

① In a sauté pan, cook onion, celery, and apples until tender by barely covering them with a small amount of water. Cook on medium heat until water is reduced and onions are transparent.

② Add cooked turkey, cooked rice, and seasonings.

③ Stir soups into mixture.

④ Turn into large pie plate, shallow casserole, or 8 individual casseroles that have been prepared with cooking spray.

⑤ Cover and bake at 350 degrees for 20 minutes (25 for larger dish). Remove covers. Sprinkle with grated cheese. Continue baking for another 5 minutes until it smells delicious and ready!

Serves 8.

Saucy Carrots

Eileen L., of Highland, N.Y., developed this recipe years ago because she and her husband like spicy food.

1 lb. cooked carrots (save juice)
½ cup mayonnaise
2 tsp. horseradish
2 tsp. onion, grated
½ tsp. salt
¼ tsp. pepper
¼ cup carrot water
Bread crumbs (for topping)
¼ cup butter, melted (for topping)

① Chop carrots and boil until nearly done, yet still crunchy. Drain.
② Mix in mayonnaise, horseradish, onion, seasoning, and carrot water.
③ Mix bread crumbs and butter and top carrots.
④ Bake at 375 degrees for 20 minutes.

Serves 4.

Asparagus with Red Bell Peppers and Shiitake Mushrooms

As a food writer, Victoria W., of Lebanon, Ind., spends a lot of time in the kitchen, where she made up this recipe.

"We have 7 acres and we grow about half of our own food, so everything is fresh and wonderful," she says.

For variety, substitute the asparagus with garlic scapes or very thin green beans, she suggests.

4 cups asparagus, cut into long pieces
2 Tbsp. grape seed oil, divided
8 ounces shitake mushrooms, sliced (can substitute sliced white button mushrooms)
1 large bell pepper, cut into thin 1-inch strips
½ tsp. salt
¼ tsp. freshly ground black pepper
2 Tbsp. toasted sesame seeds

① Bring 3 quarts water to a boil in a large saucepan, add the asparagus, cover, and boil for 2 minutes.

② Remove asparagus from water and plunge it into an ice bath for 2 minutes. Drain and pat dry.

③ In large nonstick skillet, heat 1 Tbsp. of the oil over medium-high heat.

④ Add the mushrooms and sauté them until they are just beginning to brown.

⑤ Add the second tablespoon of oil to the pan and add the asparagus, bell pepper strips, salt, and pepper.

⑥ Stir fry for 5 minutes or until the asparagus and peppers are heated through.

⑦ Place on serving platter and sprinkle with sesame seeds.

Serves 4-6.

Sautéed Fresh

"This is the way we enjoy our freshly picked Roma tomatoes," writes Deb P., of Midland, Mich. *"We also add other fresh veggies to it for variety, such as 2- to 3-inch zucchini and yellow squash cut lengthwise."*

Cut Small Golden Jubilee and Gala tomatoes in half and add them to the Romas and squash for a nice vegetable dish, she says. Add your own favorites to make it even better.

⅓ cup olive oil
1 Tbsp. unsalted butter
Pinch sea salt
⅛ tsp. black pepper
1 Tbsp. or ⅛ cup parsley leaves, finely chopped
2-3 sweet basil leaves, finely chopped
2-3 leaves of oregano, marjoram, and thyme, finely chopped
⅛ tsp. ground paprika
6-8 Roma tomatoes, sliced in half lengthwise

① On top of stove, use medium/high heat. In a large skillet, heat the olive oil, then add butter and stir until butter melts. Add sea salt, pepper, herbs, and paprika, and stir.

② Add Roma tomatoes, sliced side down, and "fry" for 2-3 minutes. If using other vegetables, cook them first for 1 minute, then add tomatoes.

③ Remove from skillet with a "turner" and place on dish.

Cook's note: If you want to substitute dried Italian seasoning for fresh herbs, use 1½ tsp. Also, if you use dried parsley, use 1½ tsp.

Serves 4-6.

Sweet Onion Casserole

"This recipe is truly a favorite of our family," writes Judy R., *of Bowling Green, Ohio. "We grow a lot of sweet onions and this is an easy-to-prepare recipe with a mild onion flavor. Delicious!"*

½ cup long-grain rice, uncooked
¼ cup butter, melted
7-8 cups sweet onions, chopped coarsely
1 cup grated Swiss cheese
⅔ cup Half-and-Half
1 tsp. salt

① Cook rice in 5 cups boiling water for 5 minutes. Drain; set aside.
② Cook onions in butter in large skillet until limp, but not browned.
③ Combine all ingredients, mix well, and pour into greased 2-quart casserole dish.
④ Bake at 350 for 1 hour.

Serves 8.

Squash Casserole

Dee Ann D., of Abbeville, S.C., took a family recipe, altered it a bit with the help of her daughter, and created a successful dish. "In our family, it is the most requested item whenever we have a family dinner," she says. "Everybody wants me to bring the squash casserole."

2 cups cooked squash, fresh or frozen
2 cups butter crackers, crushed
1 cup cheddar cheese, grated
1 cup onion, chopped
1 egg
¾ stick butter or margarine
Salt and pepper to taste

① Mix together all ingredients.
② Pour into a buttered casserole dish and bake at 350 degrees for 45 minutes to 1 hour.

Serves 6.

Tomato Pudding

Linda M., of Castalia, N.C., remembers her mother making this treat when she was young. "It was always my favorite, and when she made it, I felt like it was made just for me," she writes.

1 quart stewed tomatoes
2 slices of bread or 2 day-old biscuits
Sugar to taste
Salt to taste
1 Tbsp. butter or margarine

① Pour stewed tomatoes into a mixing bowl.
② Crumble up bread and add to tomatoes.
③ Add sugar, salt.
④ Mix well and pour into a greased 8x8 pan.
⑤ Place small bits of butter or margarine on top.
⑥ Bake at 350 degrees for 30 minutes (tomatoes will bubble around the edges).
⑦ Let sit for 5 minutes before eating.

Serves 6-8.

BLT Boats

"I always have an abundance of garden-ripe tomatoes from June to September and while I do can some for winter use, there is nothing like the flavor of a fresh picked ripe tomato," writes *Jaci H., of Dandridge, Tenn.*

10 Roma tomatoes, split lengthwise
½ lb. strip bacon, fried crisp
4 cups iceberg lettuce, finely shredded
¾ cup mayonnaise or Miracle Whip-style salad dressing

① Spoon out seeds and membrane of the Roma halves.
② Finely chop bacon in food processor.
③ Shred lettuce with a hand grater or use grating blade in a food processor.
④ In large mixing bowl, combine lettuce, bacon, and mayonnaise. If it's too dry, add a little buttermilk or more mayonnaise.
⑤ Spoon into Roma halves and put on a platter.
⑥ Garnish with paprika or parsley if desired.

Yields 10 appetizer servings.

Green Bean Bundle

"This is my Aunt Becky's recipe and one that was hard for me to get the recipe on paper," writes Lydia C., of Paris, Texas. *"It was taught to me by using 'a handful of this' and a 'dash of that,' and can easily be altered depending on who is coming to dinner."*

1 package bacon
2-3 cans whole green beans (or a similar amount of frozen or fresh green beans)
1 stick butter, melted
½ cup brown sugar
2-3 Tbsp. Worcestershire sauce
Salt and pepper to taste
Garlic salt (optional)

① Cut bacon strips in half.
② Drain green beans, reserving some of the liquid.
③ Wrap a bacon slice around 5 or 6 whole green beans and lay seam side down (or use a toothpick to hold it together) in the bottom of a 9 x 13 pan, until green beans are gone.
④ Melt butter, then stir in brown sugar, Worcestershire sauce, salt, pepper, and garlic salt. If mixture is too thick to pour or is not enough to cover the green beans, add some of the reserved liquid from green beans or chicken stock.
⑤ Pour mixture over the green beans. Best if they marinate overnight covered in foil in the refrigerator.
⑥ Bake for 25-30 minutes at 350 degrees until hot.

Serves 6-8.

Grandma's Turkey Stuffing

"I fix this at Christmas. Everyone loves it. This is my own recipe," says Bobbie M., of Burton, Texas, who has made this recipe since 1969.

1 8-oz. package of long grain and wild rice mix
2 cups cooked giblets or livers and gizzards, chopped
1½ cups celery, sliced
½ cup onions, chopped
1½ cups sliced mushrooms, canned or fresh
¼ lb. butter or margarine
1 8-oz. package of herb stuffing mix
1 cup hot water or chicken broth
1 2-oz. jar of sliced pimentos, drained
½ cup chopped parsley
1 Tbsp. poultry seasoning
1 tsp. salt
1 tsp. pepper
2 lbs. boiled shrimp, cut in pieces

① Cook wild rice mix as directed on package.
② Cook giblets, saving broth.
③ Meanwhile, sauté celery, onions, and mushrooms in butter for 2 minutes.
④ Add herb stuffing mix to hot water or broth, along with pimentos, parsley, poultry seasoning, salt, and pepper. Mix well.
⑤ Add hot cooked rice mix. Mix well.
⑥ Add giblets and boiled shrimp.
⑦ Add ½ to 1 cup of giblet broth as needed for moisture.
⑧ Pour into baking dish and bake about 1 hour at 350 degrees.

Serves 8.

Bobbie's note: I put shrimp across the top for looks.

Twice-Baked Sweet Potatoes

"Here's an easy-to-prepare veggie dish kids and adults both gobble up," writes Marie S., of Spencerville, Okla. "Sweet potatoes are very nutritious, and high in fiber, vitamin A, antioxidants, calcium and just plain ol' yum."

5 large smooth sweet potatoes
3 Tbsp. brown sugar
½ tsp. nutmeg
½ tsp. cinnamon
½ cup orange juice

① Preheat oven to 375 degrees.
② Spray cookie sheet with non-stick baking spray.
③ Cut sweet potatoes in half lengthwise. Arrange on baking sheet, cut-side down. Spray skins with baking spray.
④ Bake 35-40 minutes until soft. Cool.
⑤ Mix brown sugar, spices, and orange juice in sauce pan. Simmer for 15 minutes.
⑥ Scoop out sweet potato flesh and put in blender.
⑦ Add orange juice mixture. Process until smooth.
⑧ Re-stuff potato skins. Bake for 25 minutes.

Yields 10 halves.

Great Wheat Bread

"This recipe has been in the family for a long time," writes Doris A., of Ethridge, Tenn. "Not only is this bread fast and easy to make, but it is also healthy and delicious."

4 tsp. dry yeast
2 ⅔ cups lukewarm water (separate into
⅔, ⅔, and 1⅓ cups)
2 tsp. honey
5 cups whole wheat flour

3 Tbsp. molasses
½ Tbsp. salt
⅓ cup wheat germ
½ Tbsp. butter, softened
1 Tbsp. sesame seeds

① Sprinkle yeast over ⅔ cup lukewarm water.
② Add honey. Leave to "work" while preparing the dough.
③ Warm whole wheat flour by placing it in a 250-degree oven for 20 minutes.
④ Combine molasses with ⅔ cup lukewarm water.
⑤ Combine yeast mixture with molasses mixture and stir this into the warmed flour.
⑥ Turn oven to 400 degrees so it will be preheated.
⑦ Add salt, wheat germ, and the remaining 1⅓ cups lukewarm water to the mixture. Dough will be sticky.
⑧ Grease or spray with cooking oil a loaf pan (10½x5½x3). Turn dough into the pan. Smooth top, spread softened butter, and sprinkle sesame seeds over. Let rise to top of pan.
⑨ Bake 30 to 40 minutes or until crust is brown and sides are firm. Let cool on rack for 10 minutes, then remove and cool completely before slicing.

Makes 1 loaf.

Herb Dinner Scones

Evvie M., of Helotes, Texas, enjoys baking, and herb dinner scones are one of her favorites. "It has been requested for when we have company or we need a bread thing quickly," she writes.

3 cups of flour
1 Tbsp. baking powder
½ tsp. baking soda
1 tsp. salt (optional)
2 Tbsp. fresh or 1 Tbsp. dried herbs (any of your choice)
6-8 Tbsp. butter, to taste
1¼ to 1½ cup of buttermilk, yogurt, or sour cream

① In a medium-sized bowl, combine flour, baking powder, baking soda, salt, and herbs.
② Cut in butter using a pastry cutter or your hands. Mix in milk product of your choice, stirring until dough holds together.
③ Transfer dough to a floured surface and flatten into a circle. Cut the dough into triangles, or use a cookie cutter.
④ Preheat oven to 425 degrees.
⑤ Place cut-out dough in a pan and freeze for 30 minutes (Note: you don't have to freeze the dough, but it helps it to rise better).
⑥ Take out of freezer and place them right into the oven. Bake 10-15 minutes.

Serves 4-6.

Lemon Bread

"Having taught 37 years, I have accumulated many bread recipes from my peers," writes Margaret U., of Harrison, Ark. This is one of her "never-fail, grade-A" favorites.

½ cup shortening
1 cup sugar
2 eggs, beaten
1⅔ cup flour
1 tsp. baking powder
½ tsp. salt
½ cup milk
½ cup nuts, chopped finely
Grated peel of 1 lemon

Topping:
¼ cup sugar
Juice of one lemon

①　Cream shortening with sugar and add eggs.
②　Sift flour, measure, sift again with baking powder and salt.
③　Add flour mixture and milk to shortening mixture.
④　Mix in nuts and lemon peel.
⑤　Bake in greased 5x9 pan at 350 degrees for 1 hour.
⑥　Pierce top with toothpick while hot. Mix and pour on topping.

Makes 1 loaf.

Chocolate Zucchini Bread

Bonnie G.'s abundant zucchini crop, a little creative experimentation, and a love for chocolate resulted in a bread that has become a family favorite. Bonnie, of Beachwood, Ohio, frequently experiments by mixing different ingredients — carrots, orange zest, other vegetables — into her zucchini bread recipe. Adding chocolate became an instant favorite of her family and friends.

3 cups all-purpose flour
¼ cup unsweetened cocoa powder
1 Tbs. ground cinnamon
1 tsp. baking soda
½ tsp. baking powder
1 tsp. salt
2 cups sugar

3 eggs
1 cup vegetable oil
2 tsp. vanilla
2 cups zucchini, shredded
1 cup walnuts, chopped
1 cup semisweet chocolate chips

① Preheat oven to 350 degrees. Lightly grease two 9x5-inch loaf pans.

② In large bowl, combine flour, cocoa, cinnamon, baking soda, baking powder, and salt. Mix well.

③ In separate bowl, combine sugar and eggs, beat until well blended. Add oil and vanilla, beat until combined. Stir in zucchini. Add flour mixture, stir until just moistened. Stir in nuts and chocolate chips. Spoon evenly into loaf pans.

④ Bake in preheated oven for 55-60 minutes or until toothpick inserted in center comes out clean. Cool in pans 10 minutes. Remove and cool completely on wire rack.

Makes 2 loaves.

Sweet Potato Rolls

Patty M., of Cedar Hill, Tenn., remembers as a little girl visiting her Aunt Beakie, a favorite aunt who was, "the best cook ever," she says.

"But when I was 8, we were visiting and she said that she was going outside to wring a chicken's neck," Patty recalls. To the young child's dismay, Aunt Beakie served that chicken for dinner. "I vowed that I would never eat at her house again," Patty says. "But when everybody was raving about her sweet potato rolls, I just had to try one. That was more than 53 years ago."

2 cups hot mashed sweet potatoes (boiled or baked)
3 Tbsp. butter
1 tsp. salt
1 egg
3 Tbsp. sugar
1 ¼-oz. envelope or 2¼ tsp. dry yeast
½ cup lukewarm water
3-3½ cups flour

① Beat butter into hot sweet potatoes. Let cool to lukewarm.
② Add salt, well-beaten egg, sugar, and yeast mixture to potatoes.
③ Add flour and knead until smooth.
④ Cover and let rise until double in size. Knead down again.
⑤ Roll into small balls and put into well-greased muffin tin. Let rise until double.
⑥ Bake at 350 degrees, about 10-12 minutes, until delicate brown.

Yields 8 muffins.

Dill Bread

"When I was baking for this cafe in North Dakota, my boss asked me one day if I could make dill bread," writes Margaret K., of Dickinson, N.D. "I said, 'I never have,' so I made a recipe and now everyone loves my dill bread, especially for sandwiches."

1½ cup warm water
2 Tbsp. butter
3½ to 4 cups flour
3 Tbsp. sugar
1 Tbsp. onion, minced
2 to 3 tsp. dill weed
½ tsp. salt
1 package yeast
1 egg, beaten

① Mix ingredients well and knead until smooth. Let rise and punch down.
② Let rise until double in size and punch down. Divide in half and place into two loaf pans.
③ Let rise again until dough doubles in size.
④ Bake at 350 degrees for 35 minutes.

Yields 2 loaves.

Peppermint Chocolate Sticks

"Our family loves these," says Jennifer D., of Tulsa, Okla. "They are such a fun Christmas recipe to make and very easy. The kids love decorating them."

2 pkgs. semi-sweet chocolate chips
6 Tbsp. vegetable shortening, divided
1 pkg. white chocolate chips
1 small pkg. King Leo Peppermint Stick Candy or other hard peppermint candy
1 bag large pretzel sticks

① Melt semi-sweet chocolate chips on low heat in a saucepan, preferably a tall, narrow one (so it's easy to dip the sticks).
② Slowly melt vegetable shortening and add 4 tbsp. of it to the chocolate. Stir frequently.
③ Do the same with the white chocolate chips, adding the remaining 2 tbsp. melted shortening. This can also be done using a double boiler.
④ In a Ziploc bag, crush the peppermint candies.
⑤ Dip the pretzels into the semisweet chocolate, tilting the pan to the side so the pretzel is mostly coated. Let the excess drip off.
⑥ Lay pretzels on waxed paper and drizzle with white chocolate. Immediately sprinkle with crushed peppermint.

Serving size varies based on the number of pretzels in the bag.

Cranberry-Apple Salad

Mary W., of Bowling Green, Ohio, loves this recipe that she got from her mother. "I don't know if my mother originated it, but it's a very old recipe," she says. "It's got just a little bit of everything in it."

2 cups raw cranberries
¾ cup sugar
3 cups mini-marshmallows
2 cups unpared apples, diced
1 cup seedless green grapes (can halve)
½ cup walnuts, chopped
¼ tsp. salt
1 envelope whipped topping (Dream Whip)

① Freeze cranberries, then grind them (grinding while frozen is easier).
② Combine ground cranberries with sugar and marshmallows, cover, and refrigerate overnight.
③ Add apples, grapes, nuts, and salt.
④ Make whipped topping and fold in gently.

Serves 8.

Southern Pride Cookies

When Marcia N., of Gainesboro, Tenn., moved from the Midwest to the South, she "Southernized" a cookie recipe handed down from her grandmother.

"The pecans were not in the original recipe," she says. "I added pecans, which are Southern, and I renamed the recipe."

1 cup brown sugar
1 cup sugar
1 cup shortening
2 eggs
1 tsp. vanilla
2 cups flour
½ tsp. salt
1 tsp. baking soda
1 tsp. baking powder
1 cup flaked coconut
3 cups rolled oats
½ cup pecans, chopped
6 oz. chocolate chips

① Preheat oven to 350 degrees.
② Cream sugars and shortening.
③ Add eggs and vanilla. Set aside.
④ Sift together flour, salt, baking soda, and baking powder. Add to shortening mixture.
⑤ Add coconut, oats, pecans, and chips and mix well.
⑥ Drop by teaspoon onto a greased cookie sheet and flatten with the bottom of a glass. Bake for 8-10 minutes. Cool.

Makes 4 dozen.

Apple Dumplings

This recipe works well with any apple, but her family likes tart varieties best, such as Granny Smith apples, writes Kathy H., of Lineville, Ala.

"This recipe makes my house smell like I've been baking all day," she writes. "You know, kind of like Granny's house."

1 stick butter
1 cup sugar
½ tsp. apple pie spice
½ tsp. cinnamon
1 cup orange juice
1 can crescent rolls
2 apples, peeled, cored, and sliced

① Melt butter in casserole dish.
② Mix sugar and spices, add to butter. Mix in orange juice.
③ Wrap each apple slice in a crescent roll. Lay in casserole dish, then flip to cover with mixture.
④ Bake at 350 degrees for 25 minutes.

Yields 8 dumplings.

Kathy's note: These are good served with ice cream.

Coffee Toffee Bars

Consistent ribbon-winners each year at the Wicomico County Fair, these bars disappear almost as soon as Tom and Loretta A., of Delmar, Md., can make them.

2¼ cups flour, sifted
½ tsp. baking powder
¼ tsp. salt
1 cup butter
1 cup brown sugar, packed
1 tsp. almond extract
1-2 Tbsp. instant coffee
1 cup semi-sweet chocolate morsels
½ cup blanched almonds, chopped

① Sift together flour, baking powder, and salt. Set aside.
② Cream together butter, brown sugar, almond extract, and instant coffee.
③ Combine both mixtures and blend well.
④ Stir in chocolate morsels and almonds.
⑤ Press into well-greased 15x10x1 pan. Bake at 350 degrees for 20-25 minutes.
⑥ Cut into bars.

Makes approximately 14 bars.

Carrot Cake

Katherine V.'s children always knew when she was hosting a Tupperware party because she always baked her carrot cake for the occasion. Her children are grown now, but her cake, handed down from her Grandma Angelo, remains a family favorite. Katherine is from Oskaloosa, Iowa.

4 eggs
1 cup vegetable oil
1 can crushed pineapple, drained
2 cups sugar
2 cups flour, sifted
2 tsp. baking powder

1 tsp. salt
1 tsp. baking soda
1 tsp. cinnamon
2 cups carrots, grated
½ cup walnuts, chopped

① Grease 9x13 pan or two round cake pans.
② Mix eggs, oil, pineapple, and sugar.
③ Add remaining ingredients and mix.
④ Bake at 350 degrees for 45 minutes.

Frosting:
1 8-oz. package cream cheese
½ cup butter
1 lb. package powdered sugar
1½ tsp. vanilla
½ cup walnuts, chopped (half to be mixed in the frosting and half to be sprinkled on top after frosted)
1 cup coconut

① Cream together cream cheese and butter.
② Add powdered sugar, vanilla, ¼ cup walnuts, and coconut.
③ Frost the cake after it has completely cooled.
④ Sprinkle remaining nuts on top. Shredded carrots also may be used as a garnish if desired. Store cake in the refrigerator.

Honey Pecan Pie

"Here is a recipe for pecan pie that you will love," writes Clara R., of El Reno, Okla. "It is not too sweet and sugary like most pecan pies, and it is beautiful. You will be proud of it."

3 eggs
1 cup pecans, chopped
1 cup light corn syrup
½ cup sugar
¼ cup brown sugar, packed
2 Tbsp. butter, melted
1 tsp. vanilla
½ tsp. salt

① Combine ingredients and pour in deep 9-inch unbaked pie crust. Bake at 350 degrees for 45 minutes.

Topping:
2 Tbsp. butter
⅓ cup brown sugar, packed
2 Tbsp. honey
1½ cup pecan halves

① In small saucepan, melt butter over medium heat. Stir in brown sugar and honey until combined.
② Stir in pecan halves until coated. Spoon over pie.
③ Bake 15-20 minutes longer until bubbly and golden.
④ Cool completely. Refrigerate leftovers.

Serves 6-8.

Chocolate Syrup Pound Cake

Chocolate lovers will love the secret to Traci T.'s chocolate pound cake. Traci, of North Wilkesboro, N.C., uses an entire can of chocolate syrup to make this rich, moist cake.

3 cups flour
½ tsp. baking powder
½ tsp. salt
1 cup milk
1 16-oz. can chocolate syrup
2 sticks butter
½ cup shortening
3 cups sugar
5 eggs

① Preheat oven to 350 degrees.
② Sift flour, baking powder, and salt together. Set aside.
③ Mix milk and chocolate syrup together. Set aside.
④ Cream butter, shortening, and sugar together. Add one egg at a time, mixing well after each egg.
⑤ Alternately add the flour and milk mixtures, mixing well.
⑥ Bake for 1 hour, 25 minutes.

From the *Out Here* kitchen: We drizzled a glaze over the cake for a little extra sweetness.

Confectioners' Sugar Glaze:
1¼ cups confectioners' sugar
3 Tbsp. milk
½ tsp. vanilla extract

① Sift confectioners' sugar, then mix with milk and vanilla. Makes about ½ cup of icing.

Serves 10-12.

Recipe Index

Vegetables

Breads

Desserts

Recipe Notes

Recipe Notes

"For all things produced in a garden, whether of salads or fruits, a poor man will eat better that has one of his own, than a rich man that has none."
— J.C. Loudoun